Machines to the Rescue

Firefighting Planes

by Bizzy Harris

Bullfrog Books

Ideas for Parents and Teachers

Bullfrog Books let children practice reading informational text at the earliest reading levels. Repetition, familiar words, and photo labels support early readers.

Before Reading

- Discuss the cover photo. What does it tell them?

- Look at the picture glossary together. Read and discuss the words.

Read the Book

- "Walk" through the book and look at the photos. Let the child ask questions. Point out the photo labels.

- Read the book to the child, or have him or her read independently.

After Reading

- Prompt the child to think more. Ask: Did you know about firefighting planes before reading this book? What more would you like to learn about them?

Bullfrog Books are published by Jump!
5357 Penn Avenue South
Minneapolis, MN 55419
www.jumplibrary.com

Copyright © 2022 Jump! International copyright reserved in all countries. No part of this book may be reproduced in any form without written permission from the publisher.

Library of Congress Cataloging-in-Publication Data

Names: Harris, Bizzy, author.
Title: Firefighting planes / by Bizzy Harris.
Description: Minneapolis, MN: Jump!, Inc., [2022]
Series: Machines to the rescue | Includes index.
Audience: Ages 5–8. | Audience: Grades K–1.
Identifiers: LCCN 2020041911 (print)
LCCN 2020041912 (ebook)
ISBN 9781645279136 (hardcover)
ISBN 9781645279143 (paperback)
ISBN 9781645279150 (ebook)
Subjects: LCSH: Airtankers (Forest fire control)—Juvenile literature.
Classification: LCC SD421.43 .H37 2022 (print)
LCC SD421.43 (ebook) | DDC 634.9/618—dc23
LC record available at https://lccn.loc.gov/2020041911
LC ebook record available at https://lccn.loc.gov/2020041912

Editor: Jenna Gleisner
Designer: Molly Ballanger

Photo Credits: supergenijalac/Shutterstock, cover; Roberto Chiartano/Shutterstock, 1; aapsky/Shutterstock, 3; Mindscape studio/Shutterstock, 4; Filip Miletic/Shutterstock, 5; Bill Morson/Shutterstock, 6–7, 10, 23bl; Don Kelsen/Getty, 7; Gunnar Kullenberg/SuperStock, 8–9; Kevork Djansezian/Getty, 11, 23br; Sarah Jessup/Shutterstock, 12–13, 23tr; Georgios Kostom/Shutterstock, 14–15, 23tl; xbrchx/Shutterstock, 16; Diarmuid Curran/iStock, 17; ROUX Olivier/Sagaphoto.com/Alamy, 18–19, 23bm; Nikirov/Dreamstime, 20–21; Ryan Fletcher/Shutterstock, 22; Potapov Alexander/Shutterstock, 23tm; Andy Dean Photography/Shutterstock, 24.

Printed in the United States of America at Corporate Graphics in North Mankato, Minnesota.

Table of Contents

Oh, no!

There is a forest fire.

Vroom!
Planes can help.

5

water
tank

How?

This plane carries water.

water
hose

How much water
does it hold?

It holds 11,000 gallons
(41,600 liters).

Wow!

water

Pilots fly the planes.

pilot

They see the fire
from above.

They steer toward it.

Some planes carry firefighters.

They use parachutes.

They jump.

parachute

They land on the ground.
They fight the fire!

This plane flies to a lake.
Why?
It scoops up water.

It drops the water on the fire.
Cool!

This plane
drops retardant.

It is red.

It stops flames
from spreading.

retardant

The fire is out.

It is safe now!

Parts of a Firefighting Plane

Take a look at the parts of a firefighting plane!

Picture Glossary

firefighters
People who are trained to put out fires.

flames
Glowing gases that can be seen in a fire.

parachutes
Equipment that helps people or things fall and land safely from aircraft.

pilots
People who are trained to fly aircraft.

retardant
A substance that slows or stops the spread of fire.

steer
To make a vehicle move in a particular direction.

Index

To Learn More

Finding more information is as easy as 1, 2, 3.

❶ Go to www.factsurfer.com

❷ Enter "firefightingplanes" into the search box.

❸ Choose your book to see a list of websites.